CHRISTIAN VISION BOARD CLIP ART

by Deanna Patton

This Book Belongs To:

____

____

Your word is a lamp to my feet, and a light for my path.

Psalms 119:105

Every Scripture is God-breathed and profitable for teaching, for reproof, for correction, and for instruction in righteousness, 2 Timothy 3:16

Compare scripture with scripture

Read the Bible DAILY

JESUS
The Way
The Truth
The Life

Son of God

JESUS
The Way
The Truth
The Life

I can do all things through
Christ who strengthens me.
Philippians 4:13

The family that prays together stays together

Prayer Meeting

Prayer Journal

Answer me when I call, God of my righteousness. Give me relief from my distress. Have mercy on me, and hear my prayer. Psalms 4:1

Prayer Warrior

BLESSED

Now therefore, our God, we thank you, and praise your glorious name.

1 Chronicles 29:13

We were buried therefore with him through baptism into death, that just as Christ was raised from the dead through the glory of the Father, so we also might walk in newness of life. Romans 6:4

BAPTISM

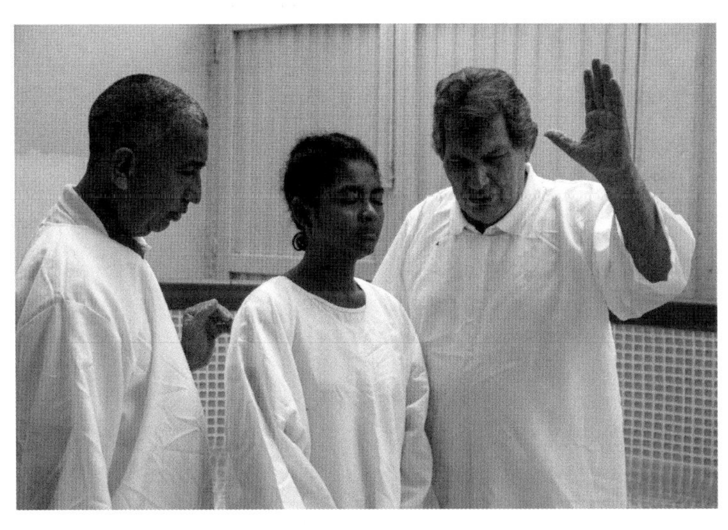

He who believes and is baptized will be saved; but he who disbelieves will be condemned.

Mark 16:16

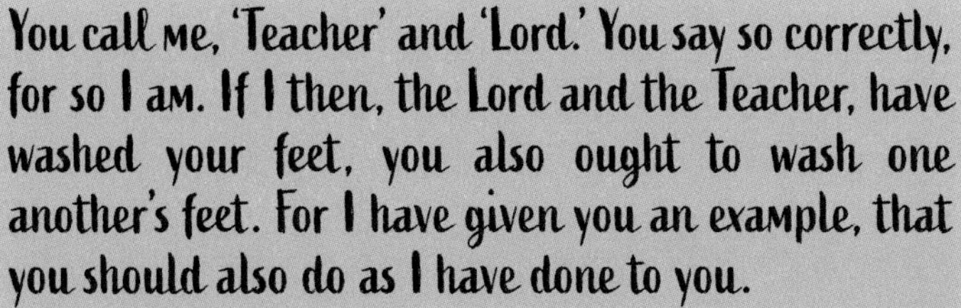

You call me, 'Teacher' and 'Lord.' You say so correctly, for so I am. If I then, the Lord and the Teacher, have washed your feet, you also ought to wash one another's feet. For I have given you an example, that you should also do as I have done to you.

John 13:13-15

When he had given thanks, he broke it and said, "Take, eat. This is my body, which is broken for you. Do this in memory of me." In the same way he also took the cup, after supper, saying, "This cup is the new covenant in my blood. Do this, as often as you drink, in memory of me." For as often as you eat this bread and drink this cup, you proclaim the Lord's death until he comes.

1 Corinthians 11:24-26

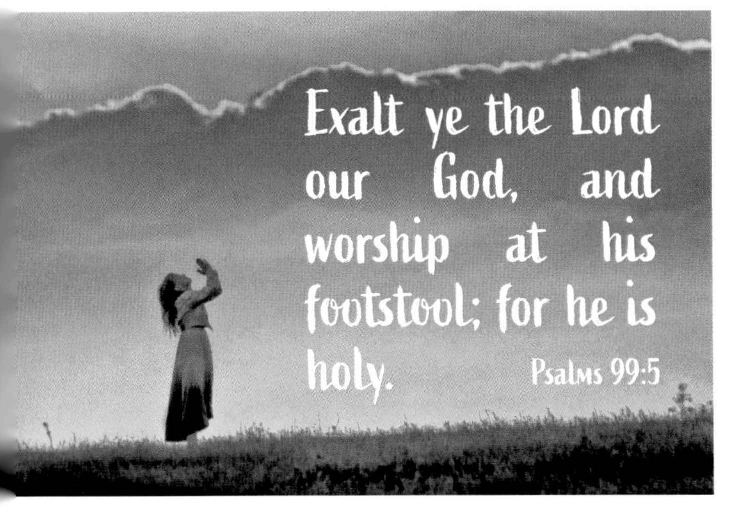

Give unto the Lord the glory due unto his name; worship the Lord in the beauty of holiness. Psalms 29:2

Sing Hymns

For great is the Lord, and greatly to be praised: he also is to be feared above all gods. 1 Chronicles 16:25

The Saviour is born
The Messiah is born

The angel said to them, "Don't be afraid, for behold, I bring you good news of great joy which will be to all the people. 11 For there is born to you today, in David's city, a Savior, who is Christ the Lord. 12 This is the sign to you: you will find a baby wrapped in strips of cloth, lying in a feeding trough." Luke 2:10-12

When the angels went away from them into the sky, the shepherds said to one another, "Let's go to Bethlehem, now, and see this thing that has happened, which the Lord has made known to us." They came with haste, and found both Mary and Joseph, and the baby was lying in the feeding trough. When they saw it, they publicized widely the saying which was spoken to them about this child. Luke 2:15-17

Now these were more noble than those in Thessalonica, in that they received the word with all readiness of mind, examining the Scriptures daily to see whether these things were so. Acts 17:11

Study the Bible

Be a Berean. Search the Scriptures for yourself to find what is true.

But if we died with Christ, we believe that we will also live with him Romans 6:8

Walk with God

Child of God

Rest in the Lord

In my heart there rings a melody

We Have This Hope

Now faith is assurance of things hoped for, proof of things not seen. For by this, the elders obtained testimony. By faith, we understand that the universe has been framed by the word of God, so that what is seen has not been made out of things which are visible. Hebrews 11:1-3

Walk with the lord

"I will in no way leave you, neither will I in any way forsake you."

HEBREWS 13:5

Saved by Grace

Step by Step

Forgiveness

Confession

God's Sabbath

Repentance

Sanctification

Redemption

God is good

Kindness

COMPASSION

Rest in the Lord

Made in the image of God

CHARITY

Great is Thy Faithfulness

DAUGHTER OF GOD

SON OF GOD

Gospel Music

STEWARDSHIP

FAITHFULNESS

EVANGELISM

HOPE

Clean eating

Togetherness

Exercise

Offering

Family time

Children

Family vacation

Birthday

Camping trip

Activities

Backpacking

Menus

Road trip

Sabbath meals

Healthy lifestyle

Walking

Quality time

Sabbath meals

Togetherness

Stay hydrated

Fitness

Regular sleep

Meal planning

Family home

Budgeting

Schedule

Family finances

Schedule

Vehicle

Priest leader

House

Wedding

Honeymoon

Sports

Salvation

Couple

Relationship

LOVE

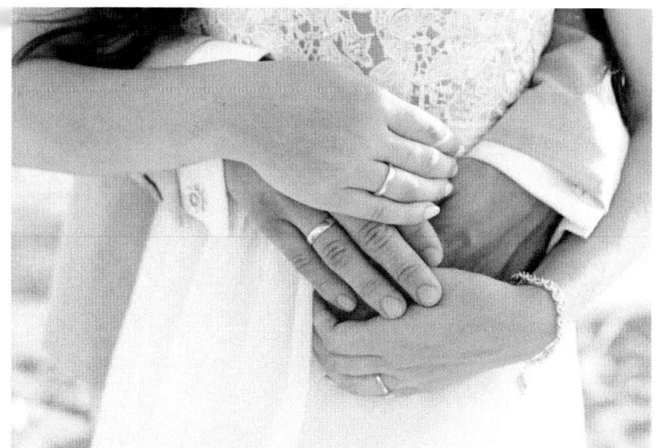

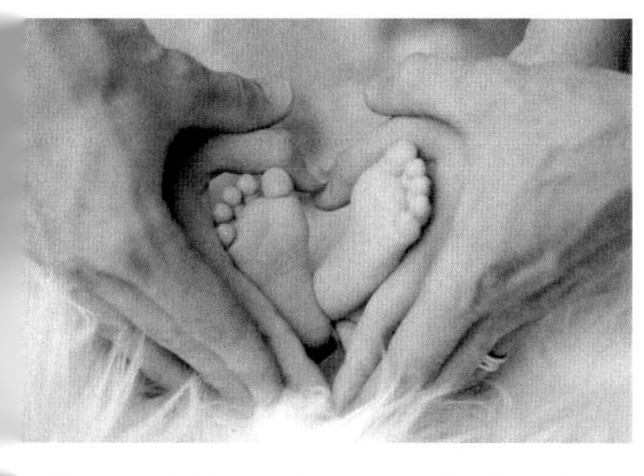

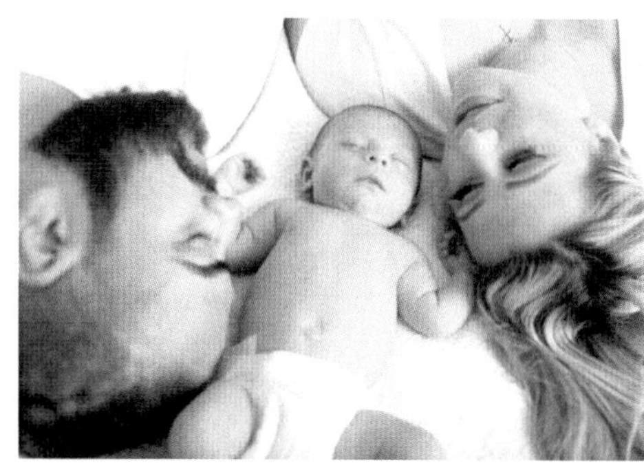

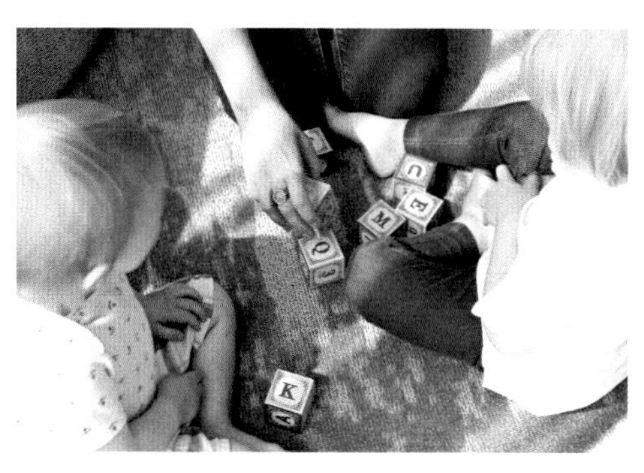

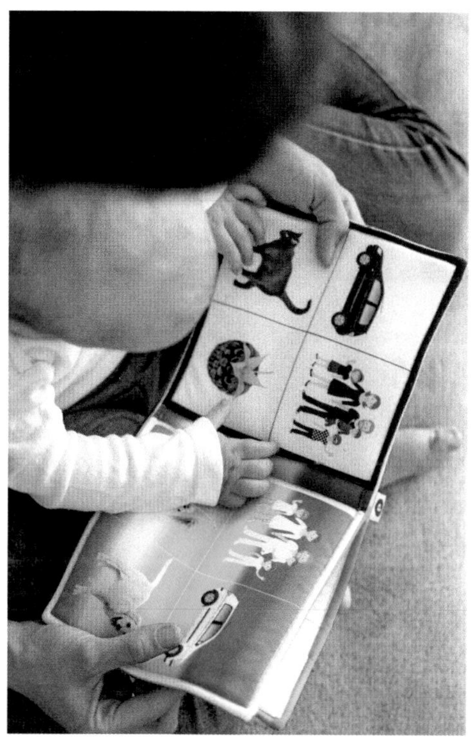

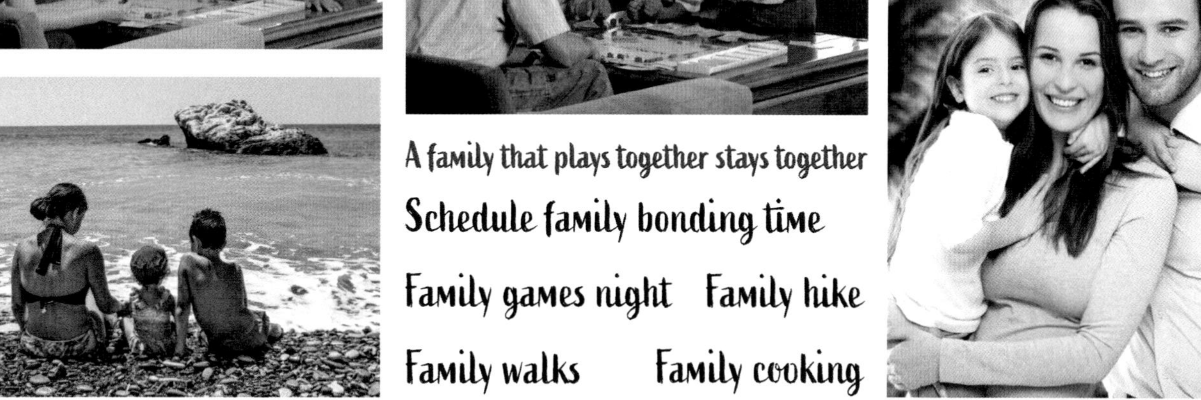

A family that plays together stays together

Schedule family bonding time

Family games night   Family hike

Family walks   Family cooking

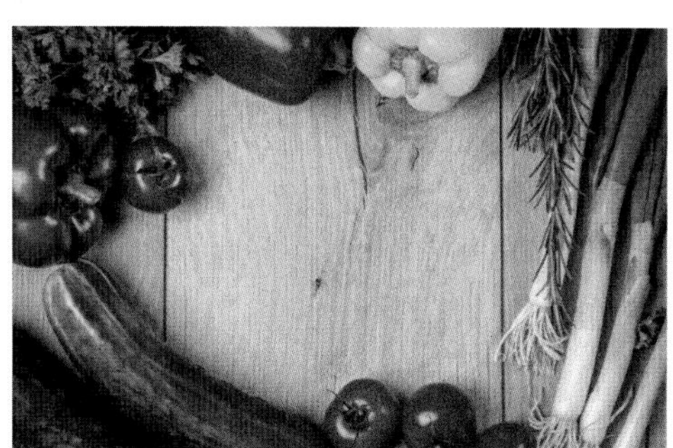

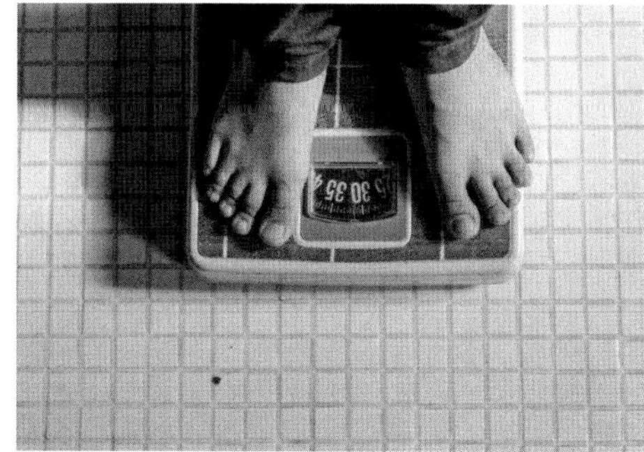

Stay hydrated

Fresh air and sunshine

Get sufficient sleep

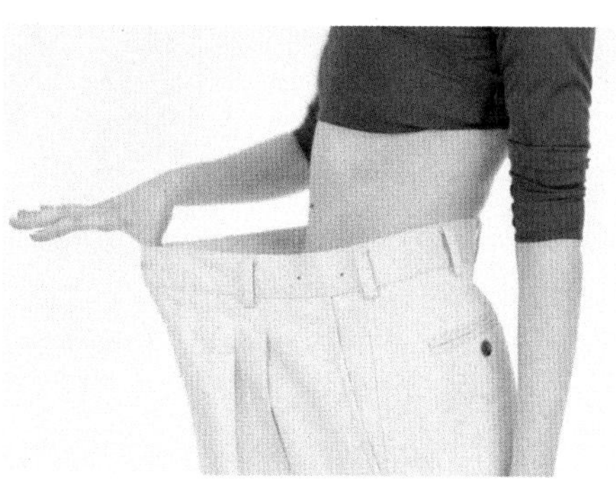

SELF SUFFICIENT CANNING

CHICKENS EGGS GARDENING

ORCHARD VEGETABLE GARDEN

VEGETABLES HERBS FRUIT

CALC

ROAD TRIP
ROUTE
66

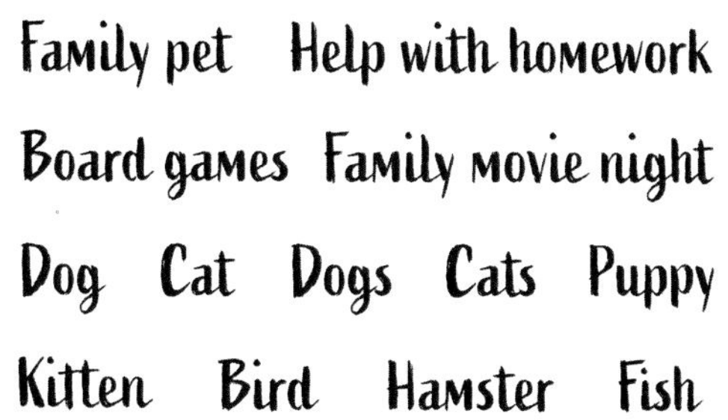

Family pet Help with homework

Board games Family movie night

Dog Cat Dogs Cats Puppy

Kitten Bird Hamster Fish

TICKETS

YAMAHA

CAMPING CYCLING HIKING WATER PARK
BEACH SWIMMING SKIING FISHING PICNIC
KAYAKING BOWLING BOATING WALKING
ROAD TRIP COOKING PUZZLES BOARD GAMES
WALK THE DOG YARD WORK GARDENING

Keep learning Learn new skills Learn new skills

Self care personal development Education

You will keep him in perfect peace, Whose mind is stayed on You, Because he trusts in You.

Isaiah 26:3

But I say to you, Whosoever shall confess me before men, the Son of man will confess him also before the angels of God; Luke 12:8

For whatever is born of God overcomes the world. This is the victory that has overcome the world: your faith John 5:4

Therefore if anyone is in Christ, he is a new creation. The old things have passed away. Behold, all things have become new.

2 Corinthians 5:17

Made in the USA
Las Vegas, NV
28 November 2024